Time To Explore

(An Anthology Of Poems)

AJIT KARIGAR

First Published in January 2022

ISBN: 978-93-5472-863-1

BLUEROSE PUBLISHERS

www.bluerosepublishers.com

info@bluerosepublishers.com

+91 8882 898 898

Cover Design:

Geetika

Typographic Design:

Tanya Raj Upadhyay

Distributed by: BlueRose, Amazon, Flipkart

Poets Note

Hello

First of all, I whole heartedly thank you for selecting the poetry book in the world of fiction and non-fiction. A poet or author becomes the one when the literary enthusiast like you select the book read and pass on to others. So, thank you for selecting my book and pushing me to do what I like the most.

I have always liked to travel and explore the unseen places like old temples, churches, mosques, ruins and visiting beautiful landscapes where one can be free of every tension and enjoy the nature and site. Just a few clicks for visual memories and some permanent clicks for life time memorial slides. Peaceful site seeing is itself and a kind of meditation for me. But when I see people throwing beer bottles, plastic bags and ruin the wonderful sites by human marks that hurts me a lot. In the pandemic situation like this we are supposed to stay home and maintain social distancing tuff time for us but best time for our dear jungle creature and Mother Nature.

It's been a year or two the pandemic has laid deep impact on me regarding Society, nature, climate change, time, lockdown, dew etc. and some of imaginary poems I have penned in these situation. After all we must give some time, *'Time to Explore'* without harming the nature around us.

Acknowledgements

I'd like to thank three women in my life if one was missing the book would have never been read by you.

One who gave life my mother Smt. Lakshmi Karigar.

One who motivated and edited my poems in all her busy schedules and received my poems profoundly. Dr. Kavita Kusugal, Professor Rani Channamma University Belagavi, Karnataka. Madam used to pick my call in all odd times and always suggested me. She has edited my poems, in fact she is the first teacher to find my work interesting and appreciated my work. I am absolutely blessed to have teacher like her.

Finally my sister from another mother Miss. Nandini Bavache, there were times when I had given up the idea of publishing the book but she is the one who forced me and supported me.

I thank Dr. Gurudevi Huleppanavarmat retired vice principal of K.L.E's Lingraj college Belagavi. Ma'am in all her busy schedule has written the book blurb.

I thank Dr.Danraj Kendur, Asst. Professor Government first grade college Haliyal, Karnataka, Sir Published my first poem in their monthly magazine by just seeing my WhatsApp status which is the key factor to continue my writing.

I thank my father Shri. Mallikarjun Karigar, my brother Mr. Chetan Karigar for their continuous encouragement, I thank my friends, family members for their moral support.

Further I thank Bluerose publishers and the whole team of management, especially Miss. Shruti publishing manager for her full pledged support.

Finally I thank you for selecting this book.

Preface

Ajit is a mystery boy to me. The boy who was so easy going, jolly and most of the times late to class could be so serious in his writing! The boy who was a failure in his Optional English in his BA first year may make me refer dictionary while going through his poems! I feel short of vocabulary some time. But Ajit makes me stunned.

He begins his writing with his expression of love for his mother. Generally we have poems of mothers for their kids addressing them as moon, sun and stars. But here to Ajit his mother is all that.

You're the sun and the moon,

I want to see you every day for fortune

You're the love of my life,

I want your love and care in my wife. (You're the One for This Soul)

For Ajit mother's love is everything. And he dreams, that motherly love and care in his wife in his future life.

People may come people may go

But you're the one for this soul (You're the One for This Soul)

Ajit finds solace only in mother's embrace. And dreams that affection and care should remain forever in his life.

His love for mother and his care for Mother Nature is evident in his lines.

"Mother you've changed to great extent,

Your dear children are in great extinct"

"Young me saw you in green garment

Now I feel your serious lament'
"Your body is becoming gradually toxic,
Intelligent creature is reason for hypertoxic" (Mother
you've changed to Great Extent)

He is worried to see the loss of green in Mother
Nature. For him due to deforestation the smile on the
face of Mother Nature is disappeared. As a caring son
he feels the pulse of mother. In happiness and in grief
Ajit never close stop seizes to use rhyming words.

Standing alone in the wild

Feeling more like a child,

Enjoying the scene for a while

Living behind the material profile. (Stand for Wild)

Very few words; said a lot in these four lines.

His love for poetry could be seen in the following lines:

Hey my love standing alone

Wearing three colored frock

With matching rainbow shoes,

Just like three quatrains and a couplet

You are my complete sonnet (Poetry)

Some of the lines in Ajit's poems make us think and
worry. They also make us feel guilty and ponder.

I'm bird; I too have a family,

You've left no place for my homely (I am Bird)

Poet's pure soul is much disturbed by the follies of the
corrupt society and the pain is expressed through
words:

The country of holy gods,

History, politics and society witness frauds'.

Poor thieves are punished hard,

Influential need one call and word.(Country of Holy Gods)

His respect for women is visible in his poem 'Woman'. He is aware of the potentiality and capabilities of women. He is disturbed for the marginalization of her victories in the male dominated society:

In the sea she has drowned

In which she is never crowned.

No matter what contribution she's done,

All those things are shun (Woman)

And the poet requests the society to be impartial and good to her:

She is the form of love and affection,

Let's be gentlemen with perfection. (Woman)

Poems with titles like 'Waiting for Another Morning to Fall', 'Music in Nature', 'Silver Cage', 'Act, React, Protect', 'Nurture Nature', 'Make Her Incredible', 'Apocalyptic', 'Mist' deal with the theme of beauty of nature and it's care.

'Black and Beautiful' is a poem about crow. But it is not just crow. Crow is a metaphor in Ajit's poem. He through the monologue of a crow analyses the hierarchy and untouchability. Thus the poem is allegorical. 'Armageddon', 'We are Cursed' indicate the bio war and the pandemic situations.

The title poem 'Time to Explore' is a warning to the whole mankind to take care of mother Nature before it is too late.

It is Ajit Karigar's first anthology of poems. In the first anthology itself his use of vocabulary, love for nature, respect for women, response to social issues, experiments with diction makes him unique. If he continues his reading and writing with same dedication and perseverance he has a very bright future as a writer. Wish him good luck.

\- Dr. Kavita Kusugal
Rani Channamma University
Belagavi

Preface 2

Here is our upcoming poet who is a student of English literature in the true sense of the term. Most of the English Romantic poets in general and William Wordsworth in particular have exerted tremendous influence on his attitude towards Nature. His concern for the protection of environment and love for Nature which have found wordy expression in his poetic compositions in this collection simply deserve the adjective 'superb'.

Deploring the gross materialism of the modern men, who have been ruining natural resources ruthlessly the poet implores earnestly to save the same for the generations to come to rid of their curse and to earn their bliss. Young poet Mr. Ajit's adoration of human values and virtues, issuance of clarion call and earnest appeal to the present day youth to develop rational and scientific approach to the festivities speaks volumes about his love of humanity. Celebration of mother's affection, feeling of pride for motherland, appreciation of the beauty and greatness of Mother Earth are the stock- in trade of his poetic utterances.

Good manners are good basis of good life goes an adage. It is good manners and etiquettes that bring dignity to humans who are the dazzling jewels in the crown of God's creation. Hence the poet holds high several mannerisms in host of his poems. His fervent wish and ardent hope to usher in better and beautiful prospective world are the flora and fauna of this poetic creations. Let this budding, sensitive, sensible poet scale a lofty literary height and succeed in his endeavor to convey his tender passions genuinely through poetry to increase the happiness of readers.

Dr.Gurudevi Huleppanavarmath

Belagavi

Titles

1. His Beloved.. 1

2. You're the One for This Soul................................ 2

3. Mother you've changed to Great Extent.................. 3

4. Again Prayers for God 4

5. Romeo and Juliet.. 5

6. We'll not see the End....................................... 6

7. Wandering Around the Wonder......................... 7

8. Comrades she will come to an end...................... 8

9. Ruin Her For Our Fame 9

10. Stand for Wild.. 10

11. Read Creed Need 11

12. Country of festivals 12

13. Poetry 13

14. Karma 14

15. Life Saver 15

16. I am Bird 16

17. Country of Holy Gods 17

18. Nature's Preacher 18

19. Waiting For Another Morning To Fall 19

20. Time is best friend... 20

21. Music in Nature 21

22. Time to Explore.. 22

23. Lives Lost 23

24. Silver Cage 24

25. Black and Beautiful.. 25

26. Act, react and protect 26

27. Nurture the Nature 27

28. Make her Incredible....................................... 28

29. Apocalyptic.. 29

30. Healing 30

31. Armageddon 31

32. We are cursed. 32

33. Mist 33

34. Women 34

35. Couple 35

36. God is Needy 36

37. We Make New Home 37

38. Waiting for New Ray 38

39. Best Thing God Created 39

40. 'It' 40

41. Present and Future 41

42. Conquered everything lost everything 42

43. Fungus 43

44. Wake Up! Life is Ending 44

45. Dew 45

46. Passion 46

47. Dark 47

48. We Move On! 48

49. Reopen The History 49

50. Royal Flight! 50

51 Stay Home 51

52 King on Throne 52

53 You're Everything for Me 53

54 Times shifted 54

55 Bee Hive 55

56 Pray for You 56

1. His Beloved

The day he saw her was special,
The day for him was crucial
Among the other star She was shining brighter
When saw her felt somewhat lighter.
In his kingdom of love she was queen of light
Whenever he saw her, said she is phantom of delight,
She had perpetual smile busy with her work,
He was continuously gazing, being such a jerk.
He said there're spontaneous overflow
Of powerful feelings in my heart,
She is a thing of beauty joy forever!
Interrupted and said you're smart.
No he said with quick confession,
And thanked the old fools for his expression.

2. You're the One for This Soul

You're the sun and the moon,
I want to see you every day for fortune
You're the love of my life,
I want your love and care in my wife.
You're summer's thundering shower,
Which bring warmth and terror every odd hour.
You're the smell of soil bought by rain,
I'm thankful for bringing me up with such pain.
You're the cool breeze of winter season,
I'm young bear hibernating in your heart every
season.
You're the precious seasonal fruit,
Available ever time blessed to have you absolute.
You're exquisite flower grown in spring,
I'm lost bee finding shelter around buzzing.
People may come people may go
But you're the one for my soul.

3. Mother you've changed to Great Extent

Mother you've changed to great extent,
Your dear children are in great extinct.
Gifted once are in great abundance,
Dear children have left no independence.
Young me saw you in green garment
Now I feel your serious lament,
Green garment changed into brown rag,
No good left in your green brown bag.
Your body is becoming gradually toxic,
Intelligent creature is reason for hypertoxic
Watching you in this position feeling pity,
Dullard is the reason for all this filthy.
I confess you my dear mother,
For lone cannot change the blunder.

4. Again Prayers for God

Long scorching season came to an end
A long wait has come to an end
He blesses us with small showers
We received with great prayers and honours.
The barren river revived other day,
Yeoman started to plough anyway
Without knowing the deed of God,
Harm done to mother by lord.
For now there are scattered showers,
He shows no mercy but only his powers,
Now the land has been flooding,
The heart of yeoman has been bleeding.
Reason for all dreadful is we greedy lords
Once again there are prayers for gods.

5. Romeo and Juliet

No words for those who talk
Both enjoy your evening walk,
Don't bother about the community
However they comment your femininity
Innocent cool breeze hug's ye' both,
All that nature wants is your oath.
Great 'Leo' said, 'god is love',
Prove the mankind your young love.
Parents don't believe your love's divine
All they know is it will end the lifeline.
Mean community knows the fate.
Have seen it and have lost the faith.
Moderns don't know the value of it
Prove you're not less than spears Romeo and Juliet.

6. We'll not see the End

Don't think that she is silent,
Don't know when she will be violent.
There are no predictions and preconceptions,
Only we can know post destructions.
There is slow and gradual change,
In this modern world no true sage
All say they are tree lovers,
No one to protect but only pretenders and killers.
All you can see is the concrete jungle,
All have spread over as a fungal,
Whatever you get free is boon
Wait for the nature's devastation soon.
Me, you, she, he will not see the end.
Only we see is mothers shattering trend.

7. *Wandering Around the Wonder*

Once I wondered around the wood
Wondered which were full of green
Was a beautiful bright day with all variety food,
Felt revitalised for fresh air and seen.
Once I wondered around the woods
Wondered to hear all beautiful melody
Melody of stream and sweet lover bird
And whirlwind which touched heart and body,
Far away could see snow spread on mountain like curd
Now I wander through the same place
Wonder to see concrete woods filled with humans
And wonder to hear unpleasant sound.
Wonder to witness the black air caused by Newman.
Now I am wandering around
Wondered to see all the change,
And wondering what all things will change.

8. Comrades she will come to an end

Beware! She will come to an end,
Aware! dear comrades change your tend
Still there is time, she needs help,
Don't know in return when she'll skelp.
All that suffering we are giving,
She'll give it back with disastrous striking.
All that we are doing is poisoning.
Watch her dear creatures are mourning.
She has made great mistake,
That she gave birth to mortal who undertake.
See dear comrades what have we done,
 Lest fight to end this with no more shun.
Beware! She will come to an end
Aware! Dear comrades change your tend.

9. *Ruin Her For Our Fame*

This world is a beautiful place,
All are busy in their own race.
Just hold for a while and watch,
This beauty you'll see is the last batch.
All we want is scientific advancement,
No one think or care about her abasement,
We all are interested in new technology
Our own tech made us lose our commonology.
In all our tight busy schedule,
Let's watch landscapes which are beautiful.
Summer, winter, autumn in all seasons,
Spend some time with her for a reason,
Don't know whether she will remain same,
We are about to ruin her for our fame.

10. Stand for Wild

Standing alone in the wild
Feeling more like a child,
Enjoying the scene for a while
Leaving behind the material profile.
Feeling like I am in cocoon
Sensing the peace and warm,
Fearing that it will not be soon,
B'coz I must go back to place of harm.
In the wild I'm just mesmerized
To see animal and tiny little creatures,
Creepy, lovely little ones with no future
Thinking about it for second I seized.
No! Hold on for a while,
Our future depends on wild.
Let's just stand together for wild
Being more matured child.

11. Read Creed Need

It's time to read
Books are meant to creed,
Helps one's basic needs,
The important knowledge to feed.
Some for knowledge gain,
Some to forget pain,
Some to relate our own,
Some to follow our throne.
This poem is a gift
Given by hundreds of those,
They are our friends not foes,
So love them and see the lift.
Read to reach beautiful goal
Love them till you feel the soul.

12. *Country of festivals*

India the country of festivals,
In one or other using unlashing chemicals
Festivals are the reason of loot,
Loot form poor to rich my foot,
Personally, love all the festivals.
Deepavali is a special marvel,
It is the festive of lights,
Teaches the peace not the fights.
Lighting of Diyas in the nights
Reaching the celebration to the heights,
Suddenly peace turned into violence,
Sound of fireworks reaching heavens
Festive of love, peace, and light turned to war
War against innocent creatures, animals and birds
To express their fear, pain and struggle have no words
Thick black dense cloud, has done harm to pure air
For which she mourns and moves on being fair.

13. Poetry

Hey my love standing alone
Wearing three coloured frock
With matching rainbow shoes,
Just like three quatrains and a couplet
You are my complete sonnet.
My love you are in folk
Attire which people talk
Your beauty spread across country,
Not only country but to whole world,
Reminding me of old ballad.
My love you are perfect rhythm
Hitting my adrenalin
Recalling a great blind writer
You are perfect as him,
Just like a flawless blank verse
There is no need to write
A poem as big as this
Only three lines are enough
To express you and ye' beauty,
Just like Japanese haiku.
When I write you lyrically you're Music
When I write you dramatically you sink.
However you are you're lovely.
You're tough to understand but
Your love has no limit as free verse.
You are my love my life
You are my poetry and I love you!

14. *Karma*

This life of human
Not a good omen
Most talented in universe,
No need of his waste converse.
I'm here to talk of fire,
One in Amazon forest,
To stop there were lots of prayer,
God heard, rain put fire on rest.
Again there are intense deep shout
This time Australia fights for life
Millions of animal were fadeout
This time even the god is not alive
To hear the cry of speechless animal
All know real reason behind bushfire
The so called intelligent who is worst mammal
For such precious work, we must admire.
We have lost beautiful creatures,
Who have not done any harm
To the brilliant animal with lot features.
Ye' all know it, no need of my inform
Finally for all this devastation,
KARMA will be the right answer.

15. Life Saver

The best living thing is a Tree,
Whatever it gives is for free.
Come lets plant a sapling,
Before we see this world collapsing.
Trees are our lifeline,
Without them we are fossils, spine.
Trees give us fruit, shade and oxygen.
In the name of development,
We are becoming more arrogant;
Arrogant to one who are deaf and dumb,
Cutting down the saver, bringing up the tomb.
We must be thankful,
For which their gifts are powerful
But instead of protecting
We are just killing.
Our lives depend on them,
We must be fond of them:
So stop the innocence kill
Save planet and feel the real thrill.

16. I am Bird

Hey..! Hello..! I am bird,
I'm not like human nerd,
I have god gift feathers to fly.
It's how I live, why do you fly?
I do no harm to sky,
You know, what you do so I won't deny.
I'm a bird with no ambition
You're humans with infinite mission.
My mission is to have a happy vision
You people are intelligent than me,
Use it for good you've bright future to see.
I'm bird; I too have a family,
You've left no place for my homely.
We are suffering from harmful radiation,
For your action created such situation.
I've already lost most of my mate's species,
By seeing this, heart squeeze's and freeze's
You know, we do no harm to you,
We are suffering a lot which you've no clue,
My request, is further don't do any danger
You're reading this poem, so be a changer.
Change yourself, for I am the reason
For I want to see a best vision.

17. *Country of Holy Gods*

The country of holy gods,
History, politics and society witness frauds'.
Poor thieves are punished hard,
Influential need one call and word.
Country with rich mineral land
We must care her and be kind,
Penetrating and digging deep into her,
Mining is more cruel and curse.
In the divine name of Ranga,
Polluting Tunga, Brahma, Kaveri and Ganga.
We in the name of development,
Losing our countries rich ornament.
Losing our culture and heritage,
She will freed but we will be in cage.

18. Nature's Preacher

Going away from house,
Disconnecting all other related boughs,
Might be two days or long,
Two wheeler, headphone and song;
Passing through rivers, valleys and hills
Could see the animal's rodent's road kills.
Speeding vehicles kill them and their presence.
Driving in absence, killing their dear once;
We carved, the beautiful valley,
Where we can see continuous rally
Continues rallies causing absence
Once full of trees, animal's, birds is imbalance
We've created a new problem,
Dirt (plastic) by human act, no less than cannibalism;
Paused the travelling for some time,
Feeling the fresh nature which is sublime,
Could witness plastic in the plastic world of human,
Throwing the bottle, gum, chip doing act of inhuman,
Journey of two day and long
No more be with headphones and song
Act of our things put an end,
Forcing me to stop, write and send,
Ordering me to stop travelling in nature,
Sending the message of nature to be a preacher.

19. Waiting For Another Morning To Fall

6am chilly walk in winter,
Four legged mate ready for I feel better,
Passing through windy streets
Could hear sweet bird's tweets.
Street lights are still on,
My mate signal me to move on
The place we're going was open,
For birds, animals and to mate gives hope;
Place open is beautiful with green mat
As we reached he stopped for lovely pat,
Could see in him the blissful joy
Running and catching files like a toy.
Place was quiet and peaceful.
Like meditating with open eye was joyful.
Sun rays are like ripened mangoes and orange.
The busy bees busy in flower change.
Further want to capture movements and stay,
My partner wants some more to play,
But there is my daily duty call,
Waiting for another morning to fall.

20. Time is best friend

Don't waste your time
It's no less than mime,
All seconds are jewels
Follow it for your wellness.
Working with it thrills,
Every second you waste kills,
Each second minute and hour
Using it better is strength and power.
Every hour is like a bell,
Reminding us that it is hell,
Work with it for well,
Life will be no less than your spell.
Every single new day
Create new opportunity and a new way.
Use opportunity to the fullest,
Time is best friend, obey to be happiest.

21. Music in Nature

In nature I found best music
Somewhat wit weird and magic
Walking along side the river
Sounds celebrity posing for photographer.
Like phantom, breeze coming from forest
Dashing and clashing of twigs leaves is best
Best of chirping natures sounds,
When I hear and sense my heart Pounces,
Humming of sweet majestic birds,
To express fullest I've lost my words,
Then there is vibrato king nightingale
Proving to all others and I hail,
Music of nature is mesmerizing
Could be heard at sunset and raising.

22. *Time to Explore*

It's time to explore the earth,
From west east to south to north,
Explore the aesthetic landscape.
For a while skip duty and escape

Spare some time and travel.
For there better seen in real,
Don't sit in front of display in corner.
Explore her, her beauty and grandeur.
Enjoy blue, clear, cloudy thunderous sky,
What is kept in mobile and wifi.
Those pleasures are all temporary,
Spend time in Nature to forget worries.
Don't you believe in this therapy?
Try it once; make your soul happy,
Time there is no time left.
Expose explore enjoy before you regret.

23. Lives Lost

Watchman is concerned of zoo,
All kind of birds and animals in two,
Food supplied is all most enough,
But the stomach of lives is half.
The owner and suppliers corrupted,
Young ones are not yet rooted,
Milk of animals, animals have looted,
 All the sins are neatly coated.
Watchmen is concerned of zoo,
Try to feed which are two of two,
Earns money less, wins hearts more,
Owners and suppliers burn their core,
Watchman is kicked and put out,
Animals wait and love rot,
Waiting for caretaker to come.
There is no sign and outcome,
Waiting weeks passed.
Loved innocent, lives lost,
Two young ones' condition worst,
Real watchman has completely lost.

24. *Silver Cage*

I am in a silver cage,
Since remember the day,
My parents love cage,
For this their home they say.
My parents say, I am lost,
Yes! Lost what may be travel cost
Travel every time! They ask.
To tell the right answer is task.
They are born in cage
I wanted the answer, was in rage,
Told me to ask grandfather.
Grandfather was happy neither.
Tale was in detail about fly,
I realized that feathers were to sky,
My only dream is to get out of cage.
Start new life and turn old page.
I tried to escape once,
But feathers did not work,
That was my last chance.
Was once again caged back.
I have forgot how to fly,
Couldn't reach the sky.
Dream remained dream
Now every tweet is my scream.

25. Black and Beautiful

I am black and beautiful
Don'! You ever think I am fool
You people read my story,
You are the reason for my worry.
You think I am unlucky,
To Mother Nature I am lucky,
I am gorgeous beautiful crow,
Eat what you throw.
You dislike my touch,
One who will give you final touch,
If I touch once final fest food,
You'll be at peace, stop being rude.
I keep your surrounding clean
Stop abusing, stop being mean,
You are all intelligent people,
Stop being raciest treat us all equal
You think I am **Shani**
In my name waste your money.
My mother knows you're the one,
Who does harm to all in ton.

26. Act, react and protect

We built humongous towers,
Showing our riches and powers,
Power on innocent and lovely,
Which they have no idea roughly.

Our world full of concave,
Mother Nature is always convex,
For us there is always want of more
So we wounded and hurt to the core.
Every day she celebrates deep condolence,
For losing dear once and her balance,
Celebrating once a year her day.
Speech, protect, sapling or else we'll pay.
No need to know by my writing.
You know the imbalance and fighting,
Increase in days of summer season,
Decrease in rainy, winter you know reason,
All my dears it's our duty,
To act react protect Natures beauty.

27. *Nurture the Nature*

For a while thinking of future,
No place left for other creature.
With no life in country side left
Gave promises which are not kept.
In future could see no green.
Humans flushed out, no clean.
There is no loved once trace,
Vanished them in full pace.
We stopped believing in almighty
He represents creatures and nature
Now we are the almighty
Rejecting ancestor who bound to culture.
Sun rays couldn't reach ground
For forests were thick and dense.
Now the rays are not found
B'coz cement shadows are dense.
Take deep dive into the present,
Save her b'coz, she is no less than present,
Once nurtured by Nature,
Now it's time to nurture the Nature.

28. Make her Incredible

Early morning and evening walk
With parents siblings and friends to talk,
Because all are busy and stuck
To mobile, which display battery suck.
Energy consumption has been double,
Pollution globalization has put in trouble,
Stop moving with the help of mover
Time to paddle and walk become a believer.
Come join together
We need her forever,
Protection is our responsibility,
It's our fault time to test our ability.
Before its late let's get out of trouble,
Make her once again incredible.

29. Apocalyptic

Waiting for the apocalyptic
Change is no sudden but drastic,
Drastic change in surrounding
Our number gaining and crowding.
Right now she needs caring
No end for our craving.
We lead towards end of magnificence,
All because of evil ambitions,
She and dear ones are praying,
Lost her diamonds yet standing,
Standing still, yet gives what she has,
Yet most dear, letting down jaws,
Wake up to make it all right,
Till we succeed must fight.

30. Healing

Dear mother is healing
Have little better feeling,
All these years we've hurt her
Now it's her time to recover.
Don't worry about corona
Stay home give her time,
Time to recover once again
To make this earth better place.
Because of lockdown
There is less pollution in town,
We are witnessing earth blooming
All her creatures out of glooming.
So stay at home for some days,
Let pass humans bad phase
After this we'll witness some change.
For bright tomorrows let's accept little pain.

31. Armageddon

It's the period of dark,
We are left with homely work,
Though we dear ones are unhappy
To some, the days are bright and shiny,
Now we know what is cage
For better health must be like sage,
We must all stand together and fight
With no religion, caste and class must make right.
The created weapon vast spreads,
We must stay in quarantine till it ends.
Tuff time to meet family and friends,
Better not now then never wait till it ends.
It's in our hand to save our downfall,
My sincerest condolences to all
Those affected by the master weapon.
Let's put an end to this new Armageddon.

32. *We are cursed.*

Animal cleaver, evolves and develops
Who stays everywhere and revolves
On earth no place left,
The animal with only ego kept.
Ego within individuals, city, state, nation
In the name of development deforestation,
So mother earth has cursed,
The situations are getting worst.
The whole world has occupied,
Virus with no end is on ride.
It has shown no limitation.
Giving mother time to rejuvenation.
It's our duty to give her time,
Pray for deceased, in name of divine.
Keep hope for everything has cure
After this take a nature's tour,
For this time do no harm to her
Or else we will witness worst war.

33. *Mist*

In love with morning mist
In my hand your soft wrist,
Walk with you is the best,
Small relieving chats are must.
Stop chasing the loyal companion,
He will wait for us he is minion.
Thinking of relationship often,
Wish to live hearty with you till coffin.
You are more like the mist,
I feel no more your wrist,
Vanished in thin air like time lapse,
Not found you in my mind maps.
Mate is waiting in confusion.
No idea of my heart relation.
How do I express she is only imagination.
Chain in hand, moved wiggling with permission.

34. Women

You know she is women
Like mammals have things in common,
Not all but some are vulture,
Living all the thought culture.
In the sea she has drowned
In which she is never crowned.
No matter what contribution she's done,
All those things are shun.
Out there they suffer,
For their identity and character.
For some she is sister, loving daughter.
For some she is beloved wife, mother.
She is the form of love and affection,
Let's be gentlemen with perfection.

35. Couple

Let's go to a peaceful beach
Where no people can reach
In search of peace we'll stay away
Enjoying the nights, morning sun ray.
Friends relatives and parents supported
For relation, with rumours they rewarded.
Found no supports lost hopes,
Forced out of fort with tied ropes.
Will never forget the bonding
Of the family friends and surrounding,
All together love gave experience different
Showing colours of society so vibrant.
Words we heard were harsh
Mouths filled with the trash,
Vulgar reached down to hell heaven high
Thought that we should die,
But my love die is for coward
Together we show lovers power,
Let's rise above all the force
Winning all the forts coarse.

36. *God is Needy*

Earth filled with cruel
Greed makes it brutal,
Closest dearest becomes enemy,
From BC to AC to presently.
We all chase wealth
Without bothering our health,
There is no end for our greed,
Our ancient gave us right lead.
Thought, learned, read, heard, from holy books,
Never the less in master mind avarice cooks.
Lowly struggle for bowl of rice,
To affluent it's game of dice.
Wake up its god who is needy,
We must help him leaving all our greedy.

37. *We Make New Home*

Eyes closed and top of hill
Leaving personal and homely bill,
On squishy greenly bed
Soothing materialistic thread.
Nature's music making calm
Thread overlapping without much harm.
Like butterfly swinging rolling air,
Brushing body and flying my hair
Gently kissing my strained body.
Sunny shiny day turning cloudy.
For movement clouds were roof,
Green was bed, realizing with proof
Wherever in nature we roam,
Devastating it we make new home.

38. Waiting for New Ray

Right now to us life is unfair,
You know we did not care.
Care our dear life giver,
We are supposed to be caretaker.
She helps us by giving all her source
Greed made dig deep with all our force.
Discovered, explored, invented and inventing
Dangerous things which paved deadly ending.
Now deadly virus has made deep impact
Spread so fast it left no time to react
Now we know the right boss
We've left no choice, it's her time to toss.
For the cure and care let's all pray,
With promise to protect, wait for new ray.

39. Best Thing God Created

Fed up of being safe
Though in these situations heard of rape
Times change relationship change father
To daughter, brother to sister, son to mother,
For such relation thought my country was safe
Hell no, in my country heard father to daughter rape,
Brother, father and relative to 7 months infant
Forgot beautiful bonds for just instance.
We are doing such worst sin,
No holy water will clean.
Witnessing such worst things,
To balance these pandemic brings.
Earth is best thing god created.
In that humans are worst and infected.

40. 'It'

We have learnt the lesson.
Scientist for 'its' birth raised many question,
For eradication found no solution no answer,
Politics, economy and society can't handle pressure.
Hunting from high-profile to low.
Don't know how it follows
Poor lives left with no work no food,
No actor, elite, businessmen spared all burnt nude.
Being away from loved ones is mission,
Fed up being in prison
No end for 'it' though passed seasons,
Directly or indirectly we are the reason.
All together help each other,
Let's take oath to defeat 'it' forever.

41. *Present and Future*

Though living in present.
Thinking of future,
Not enjoying single moment
Be amused by present, being more mature.
Thinking a lot of past,
Pursuing rags of rust.
Making the life dry and dark
Penetrating deep, memories leave mark.
Live the moment fullest,
Kill the ego it's the cruellest
Stop bothering about the friend rival.
Work silently wait for virtuous arrival.
Work selflessly in this long journey
Karma will be in favour b'coz you're worthy

42. Conquered everything lost everything

The beautiful orb is one
Here heart beats are in ton
They and we run to survive,
With no food water no revive.
The heavenly orb is one
Divided it to per person in ton
Continent, country, state, village,
To single. Wish no more turn this page.
They never fought fight for soil,
We for water minerals and oil,
Their condition are getting worse
Vanishing every second, we dig deep to crust.
We left no sea soil, for them only pain and nothing,
Though we conquered all but lost everything.

43. Fungus

With sudden plan went on tour,
Jungle with full grown some rotten
No stop for rain he only pore,
Dry no cotton could witness culture forgotten.
On the way bridges were overflowing
Stopping us so we could do no harm,
The high and low filled with green filling
Conveying us they are untouched and calm.
We reached our destiny Dandeli,
Me witnessing barbaric civic fungus
Other day on expedition went to river kali,
Breath taking Kali hunting for justice.
Warning us to be away from her land,
Stopping the fungal to spread on her sand.
It's our duty to stop fungus spreading,
Justice witness the hill, flow, low enjoying.

44. *Wake Up! Life is Ending*

Wake up! Life is ending,
Techno is the place we're spending.
Living all the marvellous sights behind
We are only moving towards the end.
Everywhere the news of virus is trending.
We all know the worst thing is pending,
Let's not make it worst.
Leave lust crust, thrust save earth first.
Look around and know history
How fast we've digged is mystery,
Running behind same time and name
Buckle up! Earth's losing its fame.
Wake up! It's already late,
Hope it's not too late to change our fate.

45. Dew

Smoking the early morning air
Leaving out everything I care.
Thing missing is a pair,
Pair is sought of dream, it's rare.
Every movement growing old,
For your mesmerizing look's I'm sold.
This morning's dense smoke,
Feels comfy where I'm in process of soak,
You are early morning dew,
Left with the moments few,
The time for me is ticking
The lovely idiot is in process of licking.
You are droplet dew,
To witness to get amaze are few,
Work came in the name of ping,
You vanished; waiting for another morning.

46. Passion

To reach the goals
Played variety of roles,
There were many obstacles
But for each had plan to tackle.
For great achievement
Need a right basement
Plan and work plan and work
Stop to like the clock's tic-tok.
Often we lose hopes
Because we're tangled in many ropes.
Family friends responsibilities and more,
Going hand in hand and achieving is rare.
Day will come the day
When you pave the way
Chasing down all those vision,
Making it as your best passion.

47. Dark

Life has become dark
No one is ready to hark.
Slowly all the livings are buried.
There are too less who are worried.
Knowing and moving to our own termination,
To protect all some taken initiation,
Rising with such tough barriers is quest
Sooner or later all the works are put to rest.
Kings, kingdoms, politics, country, race.
Atomic, hydro, bio, nuclear, will clear in pace.
Humans have created several ways
To end marvels and themselves living no trace.
Stop discovering barren and sending rover,
Yet there is time to protect beauty and recover.

48. *We Move On!*

Now, now it's the time
Time, time to write some rhyme,
Rhyme, rhyme something which is important,
Important, important things are never seen urgent.
For everything on earth is on crises,
Crises are on increase like mice's.
Animal, bird, green, mountain and more,
Everything is on lane vanishing, no one to restore.
For restoring are committee and offices
The peoples, signature, corruption are more
mysterious.
Some things on earth never change,
The earth is the one which is on rapid change.
All of us know how worst it is going on,
We care a bit and then we move on.

49. Reopen The History

Earth is no less than an oven.
Land has problems more than dozen,
Planets frozen area is melting,
Satan's influence is not stopping,
The process of end is speeding.
Sudden change in thirty to forty years.
All the livings are on edge of spears,
Drastic changes are known for slow recovery,
We are still in search, dig and discovery,
Seven deadly sins are rampantly dancing.
Finding the new land to survive,
Protect the self and let leave it to revive.
Remember the mother's old green glory,
There are lot more things in present to worry,
Seeing all these turns my heart feels sorry.
Come let's stand together and change.
Let's reopen the history's green glory page.

50. Royal Flight!

Birds are from and form of fantasy
The one which I think are mighty.
Known for beauty and wide variety,
Catch them and cage them and say our property,
Steal and hunt them from family without mercy.
In search of 3G 4G 5G superfast surfing,
They've lost their hatching from nestling.
 Only the sketch and painting
Of mighty winged will soon be remaining

In search of powerful wireless sensation
We will soon lose the winged motion.
Once the worshiper of mesmerising flight
Now to get amused we see no sights.
To achieve their flight, height, companies fight.
What so ever we'll never be such amazing,
Let's take step together and make the view breath-
taking.

51. Stay Home

Weird kind of time has come
No freedom to leave the home,
We are left with full leisure
To enjoy and feel no pleasure.
Less pollution nil is the traffic
But to leave the house feels horrific
Because witnessed man dear life's
Struggled and lost their lives.
The death toll has increased
No proper funeral for the deceased
The deadly virus has life deep mark,
No statesman properly responded infected hark.
Some of them came forward only to show,
Others hid themselves cold and froze like show
Doctors working hard to protect
Policemen making people to act
Properly. Now it's our duty responsibility
To stay home with our loved ones,
Or else we will be framed from the reality.

52. King on Throne

From mumble to talk, toddle to walk
Taught me life lessons and moral.
From moulding with chalk
To toughest situation handle normal.
You've taught me everything.
The days we went for trekking
I was tired and lift on your shoulders
To reach destiny felt like flying with feathers.
You served the nation with pride
As backbone always stood by my side.
It's the day to welcome your grandson
More responsibilities have begun
I promise you father that I'll always
Be on the road you've shown
As you've put the shine I'll be rays.
You'll be in my heart as king on throne

53. You're Everything for Me

Working from morning till evening
But comes home with super bling
On his face with no trace
Of tiredness but winning all the race
For his two little piece of leather
With no care of any weather.
Bringing us the sweets wrapped
And opening from pockets stained.
With no care for self
You are our dear lovely elf.
Sometimes very strict for studies
Solving the problems with little worries.
Hero, superhero, what shall I name you rather
Elf, God you're everything for me dear father.

54. Times shifted

Every summer increase in temperature,
Can't tolerate more this humid summer
Covered in sweat and like infants I wear
Wished for winter and little shower.
Wished for showers but blessed
With thunderstorms and cloudburst.
My heart with fear it pumped
Even the earth trembled till its crust.
Though wished for less it gave more
In return what we gave must think till core.
This time it did not feel like a blessing
It felt more like Thor's warning.
You know and I know colours of earth
Are fading, I wish no another birth
To see this mighty beautiful to be fallen
Were minds and hearts more selfish and rotten.
Now it's almost the times shifted
Earth has become humans crafted.
Changing it back had become task,
Days have come even can't go without mask.

55. Bee Hive

Right now Life of buzzing bee
Who forgot the way of lea
And stuck in a rented house
In the world unknown like spouse.
Stuck in house trying to escape,
Restrictions curtailed to explore landscape.
Flying up and down sitting here and there,
Touring with friends for delicious food seems rare.
Stuck in friendly warmth situation,
But always frozen in nature's hallucination.
Want to break rules go out taste
Delicious honey from flowers with mates,
Also there is feeling of insecurity
After all must come back to hive is maturity,
But getting infected with stinging decease
And infecting old, week, caring, loving bees
Will be sin. So now buzzing around all
The windows which are knitted,
The sun shine and cold air soothing make fall
Asleep. With a leap ahead want everything cleared.

56. Pray for You

Shall I pray for you?
Or do I pray you
I am always in a queue
With questions every minute new.
Should I thank you for this life
Or shall I wish you in my other lives
Do I celebrate on prestigious Mother's Day?
Or all these and upcoming every second, a day.
Do you know that I Love you
What Can I do to prove?
Whatever I do is almost nil
In front of precious love it's just kill.
But mother I will pray you and for you.
I will thank you and wish you in other lives
I celebrate each day and find the ans to que new.
I don't know what you think of me and my views,
But Maa I am the flesh your gift
One day I'll make your head lift
High and will make you feel proud
The only thing I can give and say loud.

****